STORIES

How God Is Healing and Transforming Lives
Among Ethiopia's Poor and Marginalized

SHARON BARLOW DALY
PRESIDENT OF MOSSY FOOT PROJECT

For more information about the Mossy Foot Project, e-mail us at
info@mossyfoot.com.

Published by the Mossy Foot Project
Ventura, California, U.S.A.
www.mossyfoot.com
Printed in the U.S.A.

All Scripture quotations, unless otherwise indicated, are taken from the Holy Bible, New Living Translation, copyright © 1996, 2004, 2007 by Tyndale House Foundation. Used by permission of Tyndale House Publishers, Inc., Carol Stream, Illinois 60188. All rights reserved.

Scriptures marked NIV are taken from the Holy Bible, New International Version®. Copyright © 1973, 1978, 1984, 2011 by International Bible Society. Used by permission of Zondervan Publishing House. All rights reserved.

Development and editing by GladBooks Editorial Services
Cover design and interior layout by www.PearCreative.ca

Library of Congress Cataloging-in-Publication Data
(applied for)

ISBN 978-0-692-24279-7 (softcover)
ISBN 978-0-692-24280-3 (e-book)

Dedication

This book is gratefully dedicated to all who support
the Mossy Foot ministry in prayer and in giving
so that the lives of those who suffer from mossy foot disease
can be transformed and so that this terrible disease
can ultimately be eradicated.

Contents

Preface

The Mossy Foot Project and Operation Change

In 2012 the Starkey Hearing Foundation sent a crew to Ethiopia to film the work of the Mossy Foot Project. The Starkey Hearing Foundation, an organization that seeks to bring about understanding between people in order to find answers to the problems of isolation, poverty, and illiteracy, was creating a documentary series on organizations around the world that serve the poor.

The series, Operation Change, features stories and events taking place in some of the most poverty-stricken places in the world. When the project directors heard the story of Megiso Meno—a man who was essentially imprisoned in his home for twenty years due to a severe case of mossy foot disease—they suggested including Megiso's story in the series.

Steven Sawalich, senior executive director of the Starkey Hearing Foundation, heard the story and was deeply touched.

Moved by Megiso's incredible need, he promised to pay for Megiso to have surgery and treatment. Soon Megiso was on his way to the hospital, where he had surgery on his feet and began learning to walk again.

Operation Change premiered in June 2014, and the story of Megiso and the Mossy Foot Project was to be aired in the first season. The series trailer can be viewed at www.operationchange. com. In conjunction with the airing of this documentary, we present to you this small book, *Mossy Foot Stories*, to spread the news about some of the poorest people in the world who bear the pain and disgrace of non-filarial elephantiasis, or what is known today as mossy foot disease.

SHARON BARLOW DALY IN ETHIOPIA

Acknowledgments

I am deeply grateful for those who have made it possible to share these stories of transformation in the lives of those who suffer from mossy foot disease.

First, I would like to give credit to my late father, Nathan Barlow, M.D., who had a deep compassion for those suffering from mossy foot disease and did something about it. He and my mother were role models of sharing the love of Jesus in action and in word and of living life sacrificially for things that matter.

Thank you, Bazite and Sitenna, for sharing your stories with Jim and me when we were with Dad in Ethiopia in 2004. Your stories were so compelling that when Dad died, we could not sleep at night until we became champions of the Mossy Foot cause. Sitenna, it was such a joy to attend your wedding in December 2013, and I am thrilled now to see you pregnant with your first child.

Feleke, you were a mossy foot patient yourself. I am so grateful to you for your love and dedication as you now help those who suffer the stigma that comes from being afflicted with mossy foot disease. You are a valiant soldier in the fight to treat and eradicate this terrible condition. Thank you for your tireless effort, your encouragement of others, and your hard work. Your story is truly inspiring. Also, for those others on our staff in Ethiopia who were mossy foot patients and now are helping those in need, I was not able to include all your stories in the book at this time, but you are a blessing to me and to the Mossy Foot work. I would especially like to mention Matewos, however, our clinic supervisor who works tirelessly with Feleke six days a week. Thank you, Matewos.

Daniel Dawit (our young Ethiopian IT staff member), we appreciate the compassion you have for the poor and outcast mossy foot patients whom you interview. Thank you for faithfully serving Mossy Foot International and for sending these people's stories to us. It has been a joy to see you develop from the time you we first met you as a teenager and to see your passion to learn and to serve.

I truly appreciate all our Ethiopian staff, who are like family to me. You are such an encouragement to me, and you show me so much love. I feel that love for you too.

I would feel amiss if I did not acknowledge the significant contributions of the late Ato Meskele Ashine, former Ethiopian director to the Mossy Foot work. Meskele was responsible for growing the clinics from four to fifteen after my father died. I admired the way he treated the patients with dignity and respect.

This book of stories would not have materialized without the very capable help of the professionals Becky English and Steve Lawson, who cheered me on to make it a reality. Thank you, Becky, for your very capable hand in editing and, Steve, for managing everything that needed to be done to publish the book. There is no way this would have been accomplished without your help. I apologize for making it difficult for you with my being gone in Ethiopia for two months!

Thank you to Yvonne Parks of Pear Creative for the wonderful interior and cover design. Thank you also to Doug Humphreys for assisting in the interior layout details. Your work has resulted in a beautiful book.

Mara Klassen, thank you for the many hours you spend volunteering at Mossy Foot and for lending your talents so freely to help select and change the pictures to the right format for this book. Helen Ernst, thank you for the hours you spend in editing for our website the many stories we receive from Ethiopia.

My special thanks to my dear family. My husband, Jim, and my son, Kevin, are always my greatest cheerleaders, and I can depend on them for their honest evaluation, support, and encouragement. Thank you, Jim and Kevin, for your sacrifice in releasing me for extended times in Ethiopia when you have to "bach it." I love you dearly. I could not do this work for the Mossy Foot Project without your support.

Introduction

The Mossy Foot Story

The godly care about the rights of the poor.

Proverbs 29:7

The loud, insistent ringing of the phone jolted me out of a deep sleep one Friday night in February 2004. Who would be calling at such a late hour? It must be something urgent or perhaps a wrong number.

"Hello," I answered somewhat apprehensively.

It was a representative from SIM (Serving in Missions), the mission that my parents had served under, mostly in Ethiopia, since 1945. "The phones in Soddo are not working right now," the faraway voice told me, "so someone sent me a wire with news for you. Your father is seriously ill and not expected to survive the weekend."

Tears welled up in my eyes, and it felt as if a rock were in my throat as I hung up the phone, sobbing. My heart ached to talk to my ninety-one-year-old father one more time, but I was in Ventura, California, halfway around the world from him. I longed to tell him, "Daddy, I love you and appreciate everything you have done for me. You have been a wonderful, loving father."

"Please, Lord," I prayed, "let me talk to Daddy one more time before he dies."

Early Sunday morning the phone rang. *This is it*, I thought. Daddy had probably died. Holding my breath, I picked up the receiver. A lady's laughing voice greeted me. "Sharon, this is Darla Lewis. The phones in Soddo are working again, and someone here would like to talk to you."

I was ecstatically happy! "Daddy, I love you!"

"I love you too," my father replied.

God had heard my prayer. "Thank You, Lord!"

My dad's physical condition improved, and he rallied even more when he heard that my husband, Jim, and I would visit him in a couple months when I would be on vacation from teaching school. We did not realize at the time how much that trip would alter the direction of our lives—but I'm getting ahead of the story.

* * * * *

It was the fall of 1945. World War II had just ended, and my parents and their four young children (I was the baby) were embarking on an epic journey to Ethiopia. This was not merely a tourist visit. We were moving to the country for my parents to do lifetime medical missionary work.

From the time my father, Dr. Nathan J. Barlow, had been a little boy, he had dreamed of being a missionary doctor. My mother, Doris, also felt a strong call of God on her life to be a missionary.

On a crisp day late in 1945, our family boarded the MS *Gripsholm* (a Swedish ocean liner converted into a troop ship) in bustling New York Harbor. The foghorns blew, signaling the ship's departure. With a band of other missionaries, we stood on the *Gripsholm*'s deck, waving white handkerchiefs to our friends and families on the pier.

My mother and father did not know if they would see their aging parents again. As it turned out, this was indeed the last time my mother would see her father. Yet my parents had counted the cost and felt the compelling call of God on their lives to go and serve the medically disenfranchised in Africa and to share the good news of Jesus. They left behind relatives, friends, and a lucrative medical practice without looking back.

As we made our way to the then-little-known country of Ethiopia on the horn of East Africa, we were delayed for three months in Alexandria, Egypt, waiting for flights into Ethiopia, which had been grounded by the war, to resume. When we finally arrived in Addis Ababa, Ethiopia's capital, Daddy went down country to reopen an SIM hospital in Soddo, a prominent town in Wolaita zone. The hospital had been built some years before by missionary doctor Thomas Alexander Lambie and closed due to the Italian invasion in 1935, when missionaries had been forced to flee the country. To reach Soddo, Daddy endured a three-day trip by truck over deeply rutted dirt roads without bridges (what took my father thirty-six hours then takes about five hours today). Mother remained in Addis with us children, studying Amharic, the official language of Ethiopia.

When Dad arrived at the hospital, he found it inhabited by many people, along with their cows, goats, sheep, and chickens.

He literally had to shovel the place out before he could clean it up. For several months, while we lived in Addis and waited for government approval to move to Soddo, my father moved in the U.S. Army-surplus beds, blankets, and medical supplies that he had brought from America. By the end of a year, the hospital was ready for business. Dad brought the family to Soddo, and we settled into life and ministry.

For many years my father was the nearest doctor for over a million people. He ran the hospital, carried a full surgical load, trained nationals to be medical workers, and did public health work. At times he and Mother traveled several days by mule into the remote countryside to identify and treat epidemics.

* * * * *

Daddy first became aware of mossy foot disease (non-filarial elephantiasis, or podoconiosis) in the early 1950s when a young woman named Bazite (BAH-zi-tay), whose feet were afflicted with oozing sores, severe swelling, and deformity, arrived at the hospital. But because of the varied needs of over a million people surrounding him, my father was not able to concentrate on just one disease.

After thirty-two years of faithful service, my parents left Ethiopia in 1977, when the communist government confiscated the mission hospitals. For the next sixteen years they served in African jungle hospitals, first in the Central African Republic, then in Zaire. Finally, at the ages of seventy-seven and eighty, they retired and returned to the U.S. in 1993. God had been faithful to them through many years of fruitful service. The sacrifice they had made so many years before had been worth it.

Following the overthrow of the communist government in Ethiopia, my dad, now a widower and feeling restless in retirement, returned to the country in 1997 for a six-month assignment with the goal of helping those afflicted with mossy foot disease. He was eighty-four years old.

My father, thrilled to be back among the people he had served for so many years, started work on the Mossy Foot Project the day after he arrived in Ethiopia. He established a clinic in Soddo and hired local workers to care for patients and to make large shoes for the patients' swollen feet. The number of patients who came to him for treatment increased so rapidly that he quickly had to hire extra workers.

People came to see my father from all over the country, as he had become something of a legend through his kindness and generosity in years past. In the marketplace students shouted, "Look! That is Dr. Barlow," and followed him. My father's life was bound up in the Wolaitan people's history.

The project firmly established, Daddy went back to the States to raise funds and awareness, and then he returned to Ethiopia to help those carrying out the work. The Mossy Foot Project expanded quickly with new sites and new workers to staff them.

* * * * *

What is mossy foot disease? And how do people get it?

Mossy foot disease is found in places where people's bare feet are exposed to volcanic soil. Volcanic silica, made up of microscopic glass shards in the soil, passes undetected through the pores of people's skin as they walk or work and enters a person's lymphatic system.

About one in thirteen people develops an intolerance to the silica. The result is inflammation and a blockage of the lymphatic system, which causes debilitating ulcers and deformity of a person's feet and legs. The diseased person's feet look grotesque and also smell bad, causing those who have mossy foot disease to be shunned by those in their community, treated like lepers. Mossy foot affects young and old alike.

Mossy foot is a disease of poverty. Ninety percent of the people in Wolaita province, where Soddo is located, are subsistence farmers. Theirs is a difficult life.

The poverty is unimaginable. People in the countryside surrounding Soddo eke out a living from small plots of land. When the rains fall at expected times, the fertile volcanic soil yields good harvest, but when the rains fail, people are malnourished and even starve.

Most rural Wolaitans live in round, straw-thatched huts about fifteen feet in diameter. They boast one low entrance but no windows and contain dirt floors plastered with a thin paste of cow manure to keep the insects out.

Half the little house is taken up with stalls for animals, such as they have. People bring the animals in at night to keep them safe from hyenas and thieves. The rest of the domicile houses living quarters. Usually a family huddles together on a mat or cowhide at night, frequently without blankets, in an effort to keep warm. Their stove is a hole dug in the floor, ringed with stones. Wives and daughters walk many miles to gather and bring home heavy loads of firewood on their backs. Most people walk five to seven miles to get water. There is little food: a typical daily diet includes a few cabbage leaves, some roasted grain, or several sweet potatoes.

In such abject poverty, people have a choice: do they feed their families or spend their money on extravagances, such as shoes? Shoes are unaffordable, and even if they were not, who would buy a pair only to be ruined in the mud?

Early on most Wolaitans did not know what caused this monstrous, foul-smelling disease. Many still do not. They think that perhaps an afflicted person is evil or that a snake crawled over the path where he or she walked or that the person was cursed by a witch doctor.

With communities steeped in superstition and fearful that mossy foot disease is contagious, those who are unfortunate enough to develop this condition become social outcasts. They are treated like lepers and at times disowned by their families.

The physical and emotional suffering of those who have mossy foot disease is indescribable. This is why my dad felt compelled to return to Ethiopia at age eighty-four to start the Mossy Foot Project.

* * * * *

In April 2004, when Jim and I arrived in Soddo to see my ailing father, Daddy was mentally alert and still involved in running the Mossy Foot Project; however, he was bedridden. He was now ninety-one years old, had been through several bouts of pneumonia and malaria, and had deep, angry ulcers on his feet. Whenever his feet were touched, he cried out in pain. Dad's foot condition further deepened his empathy for those suffering from mossy foot disease. After undergoing skin grafting surgery on his ulcers, he commented to me, "How I wish everyone could have shoes."

One day Daddy called me into his bedroom. "Sharon, come here. I want you to meet someone." Seated on a chair by his bed was an elderly woman with stray locks of curly white hair peeping out from her headscarf. "Sharon, this is Bazite." She was the first person with mossy foot disease that Daddy had ever seen, some fifty years before. Bazite was only one of many former mossy foot patients Jim and I met during our time in Ethiopia. Their stories affected us deeply.

Jim and I returned home, but later that fall my husband returned to Ethiopia to bring Dad back to California. Two weeks later my father died, a week before his ninety-second birthday. God had blessed him with a rich, productive life. Daddy had once told me that he thought his latter years would be some of the most productive of his life.

When Dad died, people in Soddo thought that the Mossy Foot Project was over because Dr. Barlow was now gone. But the cause of the people with mossy foot disease whom Jim and I had met on our trip to Ethiopia was so compelling that it woke us up at night. We got out Daddy's correspondence and started contacting donors to let them know that the Mossy Foot Project would continue.

In these pages you will read the stories of Bazite and others whose lives have been completely changed by the love of Christ extended through the Mossy Foot Project.

DR. NATHAN BARLOW AND HIS WIFE DORIS

1

Bazite's Story

He Was a Father to Me

God in heaven and Dr. Barlow on earth were my fathers.

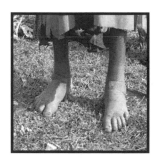

I was born and raised in the district of Duguna Dido, in Wolaita zone, in the 1940s and '50s. I lived with my father and mother and had a fairly typical childhood.

While I was still a young woman, not yet married, I noticed one day that something was wrong with my feet. They had begun to itch and swell, and skin peeled off and made them hurt. I felt cold and feverish at times as well. Headache and fever made me shiver. Whenever I was sick like this, I couldn't eat or drink for three or four days.

Instead of getting better, my feet and my illness got worse.

One day a neighbor of ours welcomed a relative, Ato (Mr.) Balcha, to his home. Ato Balcha had come to visit from the town of Soddo in Wolaita zone. When Ato Balcha noticed my feet and saw how much I was suffering, he told my father about Dr. Barlow, a man who worked at the hospital in his hometown. My father, who loved me and was concerned about my condition, decided to take me to Soddo for treatment.

It was a difficult journey, because by this point I could no longer walk. I dragged myself painfully to the hospital in Soddo, a thirty-five-mile journey, over the course of three days to seek help.

On the day I went to see him, Dr. Barlow was busy working with other patients. Finally it was my turn. The doctor came toward me, and I noticed that he was very young. I found out later that he was married and had four small children. With gentleness and concern, he knelt down to see my feet. He asked me my story and how I had ended up with swollen, damaged feet.

I didn't know it, but Dr. Barlow had never treated anyone with mossy foot disease before. In fact, the cause of the disease was still unknown.

Because of the scope and demands of his medical work, Dr. Barlow was not able to focus primarily on any one ailment at this time. The doctor did, however, know that some types of elephantiasis were caused by filaria—parasitical worms. After examining my feet and hearing my background, Dr. Barlow told me that he thought that worms, as thin as the line from a spider's web, had gone into my feet from either the soil or the house where I lived. He believed that whenever the worms moved in my feet, they made me sick and feverish. [In 1997 it was discovered that mossy foot disease is caused not by parasites or germs but by volcanic silica in the soil.]

Dr. Barlow reassured me that the disease would not be transmitted to any of my family or friends. He told me also that the worms could be removed from my feet—but if he removed the worms, he told me, I would die from the surgery. He told me that he would be deeply sorrowful if I died, because he cared for me. I was surprised by his words—I had never met anybody like this man.

After we had been in Soddo for a short time, my dear father had to leave me. My treatment would take some time, and my father had to return home. I was taken to stay in the house of a local woman.

I missed my father terribly and felt alone in a strange new land. But Dr. Barlow was a great comfort to me. He told me that he would take care of me all my life, until I died. And even if he himself were to die, he promised me that he would make sure that I continued to have help.

Dr. Barlow was a very kind man. He treated all his patients and the clinic workers with respect—everyone was equal in his eyes. He smelled the patients' wounds and washed their sores. Whenever he saw a person in need, he would take off his own shirt and socks and give them away. Dr. Barlow was known for his generosity.

Dr. Barlow was also a man of faith. Before he treated a patient for the first time, he would ask the person if he or she knew Jesus

Christ as Savior. If a patient replied that he or she did not, Dr. Barlow would give that person a cassette tape and a tape player with a sermon on it that explained the gospel. Then, before treating a patient, he would pray for the person. He encouraged everybody to be strong in the Lord. Before returning home after treatment, every patient asked Dr. Barlow to pray for him or her.

Dr. Barlow asked me to start coming in regularly for treatment. Every day he examined my feet and gave me medicine. Day after day he gave me injections and washed my feet with soap. Each day I put my feet in a bucket filled with a black liquid—potassium permanganate—and soaked them for half an hour. Then, after my feet finished soaking, I applied ointment to them. Over time my feet showed some improvement.

In time I married an evangelist from Kindo Koysha, another district in Wolaita. In many ways my life was going well, but my feet had been so bad that they would not heal. By the time I was pregnant with my third child, my feet had become huge. They were covered with bulges and looked as if they had extra toes on them. Dr. Barlow told me that one of my toes would have to be removed by surgery.

Dr. Barlow had never done surgery for mossy foot before—I was the first patient he treated surgically for this disease.

When the day arrived for my surgery, Dr. Barlow gave me an injection in my back and then shocked me with electricity. When my foot grew numb, he burned it and removed part of the skin as well as one of my toes. I still have scars today from the surgery on my foot.

After he performed the surgery, the doctor carried me in his arms and laid me on my bed as if I had been his own daughter.

After surgery my feet grew completely well. The hospital gave me shoes and covered my living expenses as well. I became able once again to live a normal life. My husband and I eventually had seven children.

Over the years Dr. Barlow continued to care for me and to make sure that I was provided for. Whenever Dr. Barlow went to an outlying area to perform medical work for any extended period of time, he left money for me with his workers. He even provided medicine for my children when they got sick. I never paid for my children's medication. Dr. Barlow was called by the Lord to do his good work.

Dr. Barlow and his wife left Soddo in 1967 to work at another mission station in Ethiopia. The people of Wolaita were sorry to see them go. I felt as if my father were leaving all over again. Dr. Barlow and his wife returned to Wolaita in 1975, and they stayed for two years, but I was sorrowful once again when the communist government took over the mission hospitals in Ethiopia and the good doctor had to leave the country.

Even though my feet were now healed, my life was not easy. My husband died, and I knew none of his relatives. My own family, of course, was far away. So I went to live in the home of another woman. Sadly, when my children grew up, they gave me a great deal of heartache. One of my sons joined the army and never returned. My son Hizikial died. My daughter Hirut left home, and she never returned. Dawit, another of my sons, also left and never returned home. Another long-lost daughter came home one day from Jinka province, but after staying several days in the hospital in Soddo, she too died. All this caused me deep sorrow.

I rejoiced in 1997 when I found that Dr. Barlow had returned to Wolaita, at the age of eighty-four, to start the Mossy Foot Project. He was alone this time, as he was now a widower. He had not lived in Soddo for twenty years. The people were so excited to see him. Everybody in Wolaita over the age of thirty knew of Dr. Barlow. Fathers who had known Dr. Barlow when he had been in the country before had told their children about the doctor and how kind he was. The children, now grown up, wanted to see this great man.

Because of the Mossy Foot Project, I continued to receive shoes and medicine to help my feet. I could no longer walk far, so my son Tesfaye went to the Mossy Foot clinic and brought me back provisions.

After a long time living in the other woman's home, I was able to get my own house. When I told Dr. Barlow that I was cold because my house was in poor condition, he paid for repairs, and he promised to eventually expand the size of the house. After the repairs were done, Dr. Barlow asked me what I slept on, and I told him that I slept on eucalyptus leaves. The doctor had one of his workers buy me a mattress and a blanket.

Dr. Barlow was good to everybody, but to me he was like a father.

The kind doctor took pictures of me. When I was sick at home, he sent Almaz Anjulo, his housekeeper, to call on me. Whenever I went to the hospital, he always let me sit beside him. When he left Soddo, he made Ato Merkina, a church leader in Wolaita and also his best friend, promise to help me because I had been his first mossy foot patient. He repaired my house and said that I should have a mattress. And at the end of his life, when the doctor was old and dying, he asked me to sit beside him and comb his hair.

After Dr. Barlow's death, the promise he had made to care for me so many years before was kept. His youngest daughter, Sharon, took over his responsibilities and continued to help me. When my son died several years ago, Sharon and her husband Jim, even while they were far away in the U.S., bought me a blanket and shoes and made sure they were delivered to me.

I had to leave my dear father and mother and my home at a young age. My husband died, and most of my children left me and did not return. I was far from my own relatives, and I did not know any of my husband's family. But I was comforted, because God in heaven and Dr. Barlow on earth were my fathers.

2

Zelalem's Story

From sadness to singing

I have many reasons to thank God. My small words could not explain them all.

BEFORE

AFTER

I grew up extremely poor, the son of a farmer. We never had very much, and when my father died when I was a small child and left us with nothing, we had even less. My mother and my two older siblings and I were left alone to care for ourselves.

After my father's death we continued to live in the small hut we had shared with him. The house was not comfortable. Wind

33

and rain blew through the roof and threatened us with cold. We had very little furniture and not much food. At night we all had to curl up in one blanket, because it was all we had. But tasting the sorrow of coldness at night and having the sun beat our bodies by day was nothing new.

Life grew more difficult for my family as the years passed. My mother went out to find work, and she managed to earn money to buy us food. I helped out too by going to my uncle's house and working for him. My uncle had a lot of cattle, so I took the herd into the woods and spent each day watching the cows. Sometimes wild animals threatened me and the cattle.

Different kinds of plants grew in the woods where I watched the cattle. Many thorn trees and other foliage grew profusely. Under the trees thick grass concealed the ground. Sometimes thorns hidden under the grass made my feet bleed.

One night when I arrived home from the woods, I saw a small sore on one of my feet. I assumed it was an ordinary cut made by the thorns, as I'd had at other times, so I ignored it, but this wound began to cover my foot and grow worse. It expanded, making it hard for me to take the cattle into the woods anymore. I went to a clinic and got treatment for the wound. After one month my foot got better, and I was able to walk again.

When I was twelve years old, my mother remarried and gave birth to another son. In the meantime, my oldest brother got married and became a farmer, and he moved to an area far from where we lived. I went to church each Sunday and sang in the choir, which I enjoyed. I started school as well, working on my own to earn money to buy books for my education.

I liked school, but not everything went easily for me. My foot started to swell, and I had no idea what was going on. I believed the swelling was caused by the wound I'd had earlier, but it turned out to be far more than just a wound. As I went from first to third grade, my foot grew bigger and bigger. When I started fourth grade, my other foot started to swell.

In order to get to school, I had to walk two and a half hours each day. But because of my swelling feet, I walked slowly and arrived late, missing one of my classes. Another problem was that other students did not like to be near me. In class I would sit on a three-person bench all alone. The students assigned to sit with me always left to sit with other friends.

One of my teachers, Ayele, saw my situation and encouraged me not to stop attending school. He told me that he would help me in any way he could until I finished. At that time the school I attended was the only government primary school near where I lived. But despite the swelling in my feet and the difficulty I had in walking to school, I continued my education until the seventh grade.

Finally, however, I was forced to quit. I did not want to, but my feet had become so bad that I could no longer attend. I stopped going to church as well. When everyone else went on Sundays, I stayed home and prayed that God would heal me so that I could worship Him.

At home I helped my mother, did farming, and chopped firewood. My neighbors felt sorry for me and wished that they could help me. Everybody thought that I would die, and I too gave up all hope and expected to die. I wished that I had never been born.

Still, I did not give up hope completely. Perhaps, I thought, if I went to another province I could get help. I did not have enough money to go where I wanted to go, but I came up with a plan. I decided to go to my previous school and beg all the students for help.

Encouragingly, my former classmates and teachers supported me and helped me financially. After gathering money from them, I went to Arba Minch, in southwestern Ethiopia, where I had some friends I could stay with. I visited the hospital and was disappointed to find that they were not educated to treat the kind of disease I had. The hospital staff told me to go to Tikur Ambessa Hospital in Addis Ababa. Maybe I could get some medication for my feet there.

I started to think about my future. Where would I get the money to go to Addis Ababa, and where would I stay during my treatment period? I had no answers, so I stayed another week in Arba Minch. My friends felt sorry for me and suggested various ideas. One of them told me something that planted hope in my heart.

My friend told me about a new clinic in Wolaita Soddo where I might be able to get treatment for my feet. He mentioned it repeatedly, telling me that there I would be healed easily in a few months. He also told me that the clinic would give me free medicine and a place to stay. I thought about this. From my hometown I'd already walked hours and hours to get to Arba Minch. Walking to Wolaita Soddo could take days. But at least now I knew where I could be healed.

My next step was to figure out how to get to Wolaita. It was hard to plan, because I could barely leave my house due to the condition of my feet. I could not even wear ordinary trousers, because they would not fit over my swollen feet. I had to order bigger and wider trousers. Life was getting harder and harder.

Whenever I walked through town or marketplaces, I was mocked and was the topic of talk among people. One day a group of small child saw me and noticed my feet. They started shouting in amazement and told their friends to see my big feet. They followed me, shouting, until I left their neighborhood. I felt so depressed. I would rather have died than be mocked by small children. How I wished that I had not come that way. I wept deep in my heart. I was neglected by my neighbors as well and by some of my relatives. Nobody wanted to say hello to me.

I went to my church and told them about my situation. Since I had formerly sung in the choir, almost everybody knew me. They felt sorry for me and agreed to collect money for my treatment. I went to my former school director and asked him to see if the students too would help with my trip to Soddo for treatment.

With money and support from my church and school, I was able to go to Soddo. I did not know the town very well, so I asked people to show me where the clinic that treated my kind of feet was located. One gentleman showed me a newly built hospital called Soddo Christian Hospital. [There have been two Christian hospitals in Soddo's history: the first was the SIM mission hospital that Dr. Barlow reestablished, which was taken over by the communist government in 1974; the second is Soddo Christian Hospital, which opened in 2005 under the leadership of Dr. Harold Adolph and Dr. Kelemu Desta and serves the Wolaita people today.]

At the hospital I was asked to pay twenty-five birr (Ethiopian coins worth a little more than one U.S. dollar), and a nurse took me to an examination room. After examining my feet, the doctor told me that the mossy stuff and the extra "toes" on my feet had to be removed by surgery.

Why has this happened to me? I thought. *What have I done to deserve this kind of punishment at such a young age?* I felt like weeping, but I controlled myself and turned my attention to the doctor. Since it was a Saturday, and operations were not done on the weekends, the doctor told me to come back on Monday, and he told me that I would have surgery and be given a bed for recovery. So I went into town and rented a room.

On Monday morning I returned for the surgery. At the entrance a young man saw me and asked me about my situation, and I told him my story. The man told me that the hospital would cost me much more money than I had, and he advised me to go instead to an organization named Mossy Foot. He told me that there I would not require surgery and that my treatment would be free.

So I followed his directions to the Mossy Foot Project and knocked at the door. A woman came out and asked me what I wanted. Since I could not speak Wolaita language, the woman went back into the house and came back with a white woman. The white woman asked me some questions and then took me to Ato Meskele, the director of the organization.

Ato Meskele told me that I may not need surgery and that for the time being I should get treatment and advice for taking proper care of my feet. After two months, he said, I should return, and by then he would know whether I needed surgery or not.

The Mossy Foot staff taught me how to wash my feet with soap every day and soak my feet in bleach water. I was given Whitfield's ointment and taught to bandage my feet. The workers also gave me big boots that had come from the U.S. They told me to either go home or rent a house in the town for the next two months.

I went home and applied the advice I had been given. Every night before bed I washed my feet, soaked them in bleach water, put ointment on them, and wrapped them in bandages.

After two months my feet showed huge improvement. I went back to the Mossy Foot clinic, and the big shoes they had given me were now too big. I was given a different kind of shoe and more medicine and bandages. I went home again and continuously treated my feet. They continued to improve, and the swelling disappeared slowly. For the first time in a long time, I found that I could buy ordinary shoes from the market. My life was beginning to turn around.

When I ran out of medicine, I returned to Soddo. Ato Meskele told me that I had taken good care of my feet, and to encourage me, he gave me the opportunity for one month's training in haircutting in Soddo. The training helped me open a barber shop in my hometown. Many people now come to my shop to have their hair cut, and nobody notices my feet anymore. I am living a happy life.

God heard my prayer for healing. I now serve Him again in a worship choir at my church. Like Alazar (Lazarus) I was meant to be dead, but by God's mercy I am alive. I did not feel worthy to talk with anybody, but now I have many friends who love me.

I never imagined that I would go to Soddo and be treated by white people. I have many reasons to thank God. My small words could not explain them all.

3

Aster's Story

A Life Full of Miracles

My life has been full of miracles, and I believe that miracles will continue.

My name is Aster Lemma, and my story begins when I was a young, innocent girl.

When I was fifteen years old, a man asked me to marry him. I agreed, having no thought about what might happen in the future. At that time I was energetic, strong, and full of courage.

41

Unfortunately, my circumstances began to change after my marriage. My feet began to itch, and odd growths appeared on them. My feet began to ooze a horrible-smelling liquid. The stench was awful. I could barely stand it, and it was a terrible embarrassment to me. But my feet continued to swell. Meanwhile, as the condition worsened, I grew progressively weaker.

Seeing this, my husband's behavior toward me changed. He had loved me when we were first married, but now he began to hate me. His words wounded me deeply. My husband told one of my neighbors, "My chickens and my wife are the same. She does nothing and is worthless."

I felt so ashamed.

At the same time that my feet were swelling bigger and bigger, I was also pregnant with our first child. My feet got worse and worse and smelled terrible. Finally my husband said to me, "If you give birth to a boy, he can stay in your place and help me farm, but if you give birth to a girl, then you and she will be out of this house."

The day after I gave birth to our daughter, my husband threw me out. Sobbing and still weak from childbirth, I trudged with my baby to my uncle's house. I lived there for quite a while, but my uncle too was a heartless man. Embarrassed at the condition of my feet, he would not allow me to go outside. He was very cruel.

As the condition of my feet grew progressively worse, I could no longer walk but had to crawl on my hands and knees. My child was growing, and I became a poor, helpless, forsaken woman. Forsaken by my husband, my uncle, and all my relatives.

Since I turned out to be more of a burden than a helpful relative to my uncle, he decided to throw me out of his house. He shouted angrily at me, "You are no help to me or to anybody else because you can't work or go to market. I am going to throw you over the cliff into the big river behind our house, and then I'll be free forever of the trouble that you are to me."

"Please, please let me live until Wednesday," I pleaded. "Don't let me die this way. Wait until Wednesday, and either you will find me dead and can then throw my lifeless body into the river, or I will have gotten out of your house on my own." So he relented and gave me the chance to live until Wednesday.

I knew that my only hope was Jesus Christ. [Wolaita is a predominantly Christian area—many people attend church and have a knowledge of the Scriptures.] In my impossible circumstances, I put my full trust in Him. I spent day and night crying out to the Lord to rescue me, begging Jesus to either let me die or to help me so that I could run away and escape my cruel uncle before he laid his hands on me.

Tuesday night I was still mourning and praying to the Lord when I saw a vision. Two people appeared from nowhere with open Bibles, one to my right and one to my left. They started reading the Bible aloud in a slow, understandable way.

Suddenly I was surrounded by a sharp, bright light coming from a cloud. Through the light I saw a tall man with a kind and friendly face.

"Save me, Jesus," I cried.

"My child, don't worry," Jesus said to me. "I will rescue you from all your troubles. I am here to comfort you and to help you through your problems. Tomorrow you and your daughter

43

will walk out of this house," the friendly figure told me, and I believed Him.

Right after this message, the people reading the Bible and the bright figure vanished, but then another man appeared in my vision. He was an elderly man whom I had known at my church when I had lived with my husband. This man approached me and stood in front of me, exactly where the friendly figure in white had been.

"Who was that man talking to you?" he asked. "What did He say?"

"It was Jesus Christ. I begged Him to rescue me from my uncle, and Jesus promised to save me from him. He told me that I would be able to walk tomorrow morning," I replied.

The next morning, believing that I could walk, I stood up and took one step forward, then another, and another. My feet were not yet healed, but I was able to walk. "*I can walk!*" I exclaimed joyfully to myself. Early that Wednesday morning, before anybody woke up, I climbed into a coffee tree, collected coffee beans, and made coffee for the family.

I had heard of some white people in the Bale area who taught people, gave treatments to the sick, and provided shoes for the poor. Bale was about nine miles away from where I had been born, so I decided to find this place and see if I could get help.

Early Wednesday morning I started walking to Bale. My little girl followed me. This place, a weekly clinic run by the Mossy Foot Project, was located beyond the mountain in my area, so the trip was tiring and challenging. Fortunately I owned nothing, so I didn't have anything to carry. How happy I was to be free at last. My belief and trust in the Lord took away my worries.

While making my way along the long, rocky, mountainous trail, a man I didn't know stopped me, saying that he was a pastor of a church. He took forty birr (about two U.S. dollars) out of his pocket and gave it to me. With that kind gift, I was able to buy food for my child and me, and we continued on our way to the Mossy Foot clinic in Bale.

Finally, after walking two days, we arrived at the town of Bale. I knew a woman from my area who lived in Bale, so I searched for her. When I found her, I told her about my husband and my uncle, and she allowed me to live with her.

Eagerly I waited for the day of the Mossy Foot clinic. I could hardly wait to show the workers my feet and to be treated. When I told the clinic workers my story, they felt sorry for me. They cleaned my feet thoroughly and then had me soak them for about half an hour in a bucket of water and a little bleach. Next they massaged my feet with Whitfield's ointment and wrapped my swollen feet with elastic bandages. The staff gave me a pair of large leather shoes, a pair of socks, and a treatment kit, and they taught me how to care for my feet every day and to elevate them at night. They told me to do this every day and to return the following week on clinic day.

I followed the instructions faithfully every day. To me, skipping, missing, or stopping my treatment would be the same as denying Jesus, because both would lead me to death. As I continued the treatment, I regained my strength.

My child and I continued to struggle for a living in a strange land where we had no relatives. The woman I lived with gave me a goat to raise and told me that when I sold it, half the profit would be mine. I was able to buy a second goat, and it gave birth to two babies. But the woman did not keep her bargain. Instead of allowing me to sell the goat she'd given me, she took all the goats for herself. Meanwhile, I made injera (Ethiopian bread) for people and earned ten birr (about fifty cents) a day to buy food for me and my daughter.

The Mossy Foot workers and the government noticed my many problems, and they kindly gave me a small piece of land and built a one-room house for me to live in with my child. Even though our home is small, we are happy living in our own house. I work in my garden raising corn and sweet potatoes.

My life has been full of miracles, and I believe that miracles will continue. The Lord is with me, so I have nothing to fear.

Praise the Lord!

4

Megiso's Story

Set Free from Prison

God had a plan to meet my need.

BEFORE

AFTER

I was born in a remote area of Wolaita. I never had the opportunity to attend school, but through hard work and creativity I was able to become a successful farmer. I also grew and traded coffee. Because I had money and was strong, my neighbors respected me, and I had a busy, active life at the marketplace.

From time to time a woman named Ayelech bought coffee from me and resold it. She was a well-known businesswoman in the area who traded coffee, false banana dough, salt, and spices. As I got to know Ayelech, I was impressed by her business skills and character. Soon I asked her to marry me.

Ayelech agreed. We married and began a happy life together. Eventually we had five children—three boys and two girls. I made sure that all our children attended school.

A few years after the birth of our first daughter, our happy life took a bad turn. I had always walked from place to place to do my work. One day, when I returned from the market, my right foot became itchy, and I felt cold and shaky. When I scratched my foot, it began to swell. The swelling gradually increased and made me so uncomfortable that walking became difficult. In addition to the swelling and pain, my feet smelled terrible. Soon I stopped going to the market, although I still worked in my garden and participated in local events.

Two years after becoming sick and after a second son had been born to us, my condition became so bad that I could not work or take care of our home. I could only crawl out of the house to warm up in the sun.

At first, church members and neighbors carried me to different clinics and health centers. But as my sickness grew worse, people grew weary of helping.

My family lived in a small dwelling on a lush, sparsely populated hillside. Our farmland sprawled over a steep slope, making farming challenging for someone in the best of health. Due to my condition, my wife and children tilled the soil in order to provide for our family.

Throughout the challenges and difficulties, my wife, Ayelech, comforted and loved me. Some of her relatives and friends pressed her to leave me and return to her father's house. But Ayelech refused, telling them that she had given her word on her wedding day never to leave her husband until death. She tried to help me find local medicines, but none of them helped.

I did not give up searching for help. I heard about a man named Dr. Kelemu Desta, who worked at a hospital in Soddo, treating people like me with medicine and operating on their feet.

By growing and selling avocados, I was able to save the sixty birr (about three U.S. dollars) that I needed to pay for treatment in Soddo. Early one morning I took a bus to Soddo by myself and arrived at the bus station. I paid six birr (about thirty cents) for a buggy cart owner to take me to Soddo Christian Hospital, where Dr. Kelemu worked. Once I got there, however, I didn't know what to do. I had never been to a hospital, and everything was new and strange. As night approached at the end of the first day, the hospital guards told me that I needed to leave the hospital compound.

Some kind people showed me a place where I could stay overnight. For three days I stayed near the hospital, hoping to meet Dr. Kelemu, but I was never able to see him. When I had spent almost all my money, I got on a bus and went sadly home in defeat.

After returning home my feet grew progressively worse. I was often ill. Year after year, more bulges grew on my feet. Due to the horrible condition of my feet, I never left my house. I felt like a prisoner in my home.

Then a Mossy Foot clinic opened in the Koyo area, not far from where we lived. An official who had heard about the clinic came to my house and told me about the new project. Because I was unable to walk to Koyo, on the day the clinic opened, Ayelech went to Koyo for me and got soap, bleach, and Whitfield's ointment for my treatment.

Soon the Mossy Foot clinic workers at the Koyo site began visiting patients at home, and one rainy day they visited our home. During the visit the workers were distressed when they saw rain pouring through our roof and flooding our home. They were concerned for my family and me, and they told me that the dampness of our home and our poor living conditions contributed to my sickness.

The Mossy Foot Project had begun a new program of building houses for needy patients, and the clinic workers decided that my family should be considered for a new house. The houses were built by a combination of resources provided by the Mossy Foot Project and the local community and churches.

Young people from our church came to our house and cut trees and dug the foundation for a new house. Mossy Foot provided supplies such as corrugated roofing, nails, windows, and doors as well as payment for the carpenters. With the new materials the church members built a new, strong house for me and my family.

I was thankful for this blessing, but because of my diseased feet, I still felt imprisoned. I dreamed of walking long distances and participating again in society. My feet had grown so large that only surgery could correct them. The ointment and bleach that my wife brought from the clinic removed the bad smell but not the swelling and bulges.

But God had a plan to meet my need. One day a film crew came to record how the Mossy Foot Project was helping people in Ethiopia. They were creating a film on organizations that serve the poor. The project directors wanted to include my story in the movie. When the director of the organization, Steven Sawalich, heard my story, he felt compassion for me and promised to help me by paying for me to have surgery and treatment.

Within a few months, I was on my way to Soddo Christian Hospital for surgery to remove the bulges and tumors from my feet—and this time I would know what to do when I got there! My faithful wife "Ayelech" stayed with me in the hospital, encouraging and helping me when I couldn't help myself.

Soon after the surgery I learned to walk again with the help of a walker. I received post-operative care from Feleke, one of Mossy Foot's wound-care and lymphatic specialists. My wounds began to heal.

I am thankful to God for providing so many people to help me when I could do nothing for myself. I was a prisoner in my home for many years, and now I can finally look forward to leading a normal life and caring for my family. I have been set free, and I want to serve others with the hope that I have been given.

5

Sitenna's Story

Never Quit Believing

God has done such great things in my life that I can never repay Him for His goodness.

BEFORE

AFTER

I was born in southern Ethiopia in the district of Gofa. Most of my life has been difficult and painful. But God has been faithful to bring me through much sorrow to a place of joy.

When I was only seven, my father died. Soon after his death my mother married another man from our neighborhood and went to live with him. She hoped this would help her get food, since her new husband would farm her land. I was left with my little sister at my mother's old house. At first my five brothers were also there with us, but some of them found jobs, and others married and moved out. Eventually only my sister and I were left in the house.

Our mother told us that she was close by and would come and see us often. We lived this way for two years, our mother visiting in the evenings, until her new husband told her that he would no longer help both my sister and me but would only look after one or the other of us. So my mother arranged for me to live with another woman, and she took my little sister home with her.

The woman with whom I lived gave me much work to do. For two years I carried water, cleaned her house, and cleaned cattle stalls.

Then one day this woman told me to go and visit my mother. I didn't want to, because my mother's husband was not a kind man. "No," I told her. "Don't make me go. My mother's husband won't want to see me." The lady told me to go anyway, and she gave me a few coins and some sorghum to take to my sister.

When I arrived at the house, my mother had gone to the market, and only my little sister and my mother's husband were there. I decided to wait outside until my mother returned. But my mother's husband saw me. He came out and asked me, "Why did you come here?"

"To see my mother," I replied.

He went back in without another word.

My sister came out and asked me, "Did you bring sorghum? Come inside. Let's prepare it." While we were cooking, my mother's husband came over and asked me, "Did you come here to live?" I did not reply. He circled several times, looking angry.

My mother arrived home that evening, and her husband yelled at her, "Either you take this girl out of this house, or you get out now."

I spoke up. "I came only to see my mother—I will be gone tomorrow." But he wouldn't listen to me or to my mother's pleading, so my mother took me to my brother who lived nearby and left me there.

When he saw me, my brother asked, "Why did you leave the lady's house? Didn't you know that your mother's husband would not let you in his house? I won't let you in my house either. Get out of here! Let the hyenas eat you."

I ran back to my mother, crying. When I told her what my brother had said, we cried together.

My mother had a friend in Gofa who lived near her. She took me to her friend's house and asked the woman to let me stay with her for the night. The woman let me in and asked me what had happened. After she heard my story, she told me that she was going to the district of Wolaita in the morning.

"Why don't you come along and work for me?" she said.

In the morning I talked with my mother about her invitation.

"Is this really what you want to do?" she asked.

I didn't see that I had any choice, so I said it was. My mother made the woman promise to care for me as if I were one of her own daughters. The woman promised, so I went to Wolaita with her. I was eleven years old.

Kind people had told me about Jesus Christ and His Word, so I knew that God had a big plan in allowing my circumstances.

As I traveled with the woman to Wolaita, I thought about the story of Joseph. Joseph had also been carried off into servitude, but all along God intended to exalt him to a place of authority. I hoped my story would be like Joseph's.

When we arrived in Wolaita zone, in the town of Gesuba, my mother's friend took me to live with another woman who was almost ready to give birth. I stayed with this woman and cared for her baby. The woman was not kind. She hit me and called me names, and I was not happy with her. I cut grass for the cows, watched the cattle in the field, fetched water, and cleaned the house. When the woman's children grew older and went to school, I led the cows to the fields and stayed with them the whole day. I had no shoes, so I never wore any.

One day when I was fifteen years old, one of my feet began to itch. I told the woman I worked for about it. She asked me what had happened, but I didn't know.

A few days after my foot began to itch, it started to swell. Soon puss began leaking from my foot, and mossy growths emerged. I continued watching the cows, but after another week my other foot started to itch and swell. *What is happening, and what shall I do?* I thought.

Before I developed mossy foot, I had slept in the house with the woman's children. But when my feet became sick, the woman told me to sleep with the cows. She was afraid that the disease would pass to her own children.

By the time I was eighteen, I could barely walk and could no longer take the cows to the fields. The woman found someone else to do this job. The woman had a small shop where she sold injera, Ethiopian bread. She taught me how to make bread, and

I worked in the shop all day. But my feet continued to grow worse with open sores.

One day the woman I had been living with said to me, "Sitenna, when people see you, they do not want to come to my shop, so I am losing business. On market days I want you to stay in the kitchen. Do not let anyone see you."

When I heard this, I felt very sad. But I said to myself, *God has a day for me.*

So on Mondays, which were market days in Gesuba, I stayed in the kitchen, hiding my face from the woman's customers. At the end of each market day, when everyone was gone, I went into the kitchen to wash the plates.

After a year of baking injera, the woman sent me to her mother's house to work.

The old woman told me that if I could not bake injera, I should fetch water for her and for her daughter's shop. I carried water from the river in a big pot. Since Mondays were market days, on Sundays I had to fetch eight pots of water for baking injera and wat (stew eaten with injera).

By this time my mother had grown old, and I wanted to see her again before she died. Yet I was not allowed to go anywhere and always had work to do. In the eight years I lived with this woman, she never bought me a dress or a pair of shoes.

I had been told that Jesus Christ heals all kinds of diseases, and when kind people invited me to church, I went one Christmas day. The preacher talked about a verse from the book of Matthew: Jesus said, "Come to me, all of you who are weary and carry heavy burdens, and I will give you rest" (11:28, NIV). This verse applied to me in my weakness, and my heart was touched. From then on I went to church whenever I could, and I believed that I would be healed.

However, even in church I sat in a corner so that no one would be disturbed by the smell of my feet. I wore a long dress so that no one could see them either, since whenever someone sat next to me and noticed my feet, he or she got up and chose a different place. After the sermon each week I left before the congregation finished saying the Lord's Prayer.

One day when I came home from church, the woman I worked for met me outside. "Where have you been the whole day?" she demanded.

"I went to church," I said.

She exclaimed, "Church ends in the morning! You were gone the whole day!"

I told her I had gone to a friend's house after church.

"I don't want you in my house anymore," she told me. "You grew up in my house and learned everything you know from me, but now you do whatever you want. See if anyone else will take you in as I did!"

I begged her to let me in and told her that I would not make the same mistake again. "I don't know anywhere else to go," I said.

She relented and let me in, but not because of my pleading. She knew that she would have no one to fetch water and help her if I left.

After this we had this conversation many times. She accused me of making her customers leave because of my feet and the bad smell. She too avoided me, and she didn't want anybody to see me. I was very unhappy. I even considered killing myself, but I thought, *Who will bury my body if I die?* I grew weaker and weaker.

One day the woman said, "This Jesus you talk about, why does He not save you? No one at church wants to sit with you."

"I know that He will save me one day. Please don't stop me from going to church," I replied.

One day the woman began shouting and cursing at me, and she told me to get out of her house for good. This time I did not beg to stay. I picked up my mattress with one hand and carried my clothes in the other, and I left her house. "If you find me dead, please bury me," I told her as I left.

I asked a friend from church if I could stay with her. My church was constructing a new building, so I volunteered to help by carrying stone, sand, water, and wood. I made the decision to live or die working in the house of God. The foreman of the project, a man named Simon, noticed how hard I worked. One day he called me over and asked me about myself. I told him how I had come from Gofa and lived with and worked for several women.

Simon was a kind man, and he was compassionate toward me. He told me that I might find help at another place in Wolaita, in Soddo, where they provided treatment and shoes for people with feet like mine. Simon asked me if I wanted to go there, and I told him yes. He told me that he would see what kind of help he could find for me.

Simon went to the church elders and pleaded for help for me. He told them that he couldn't continue working unless they agreed to give me help. The elders listened, and after discussion they agreed to help by collecting money for me to go to Soddo.

Simon came and told me the next morning that I would be going to the Otona Government Hospital (formerly the SIM mission hospital in Soddo).

When Simon and I arrived at the hospital, Dr. Kelemu examined me and felt very concerned for me. He took my picture and told me that he would operate on one of my feet the next day. Dr. Kelemu told Simon that he could return home, but Simon did not want to leave me. He said that bringing me to the hospital was his responsibility. Simon stayed in Soddo for three weeks while I recovered from surgery on my first foot. Every month after that he collected money and brought it to me from my church in Gesuba.

A month after my first surgery, one foot was healed, and I was ready for surgery on the other foot. I spent nine months in the hospital altogether and left with both of my feet nearly healed. When I returned to Gesuba, Simon invited me to stay with him until my feet were well enough for me to work.

When the woman I had worked for heard that I had returned from Soddo, she came to visit me. She asked me if I wanted to come live with her, but I told her that I was happy at Simon's. After a year at Simon's house, my feet were healed, and Simon suggested that I rent a small house for myself. I agreed, and I earned money for food and rent by braiding women's hair and baking injera. But it was a struggle to make enough money, especially to buy the new shoes I needed.

One day when I was worrying about how I would buy my shoes, I remembered something that Dr. Kelemu had said to me. He had told me that because I had suffered so much, he would help me find a job when I got well. Dr. Kelemu was a compassionate man. He had even given me one hundred birr (about five U.S. dollars) before I came back to Gesuba.

As I thought about Dr. Kelemu's kindness, I decided to return to Soddo to find him and ask him about a job. Dr. Kelemu told me that he didn't know of a job but that he would talk with Ato Meskele, the director of the Mossy Foot Project, and let me know in a week. Until then he said that I could stay in the hospital compound with the patients.

When I came back to him, Dr. Kelemu told me, "Sitenna, I have not been able to talk with Ato Meskele yet, but I have another idea. I want you to go and tell your story to Dr. Barlow, the founder of Mossy Foot. Don't tell him that I sent you—just tell him your story, and see what he says."

With some anxiety I went and knocked on Dr. Barlow's door. "*Gala* [come in]," he said, and I entered. Dr. Barlow asked me why I had come, and I told him everything.

Dr. Barlow listened intently to all I said. "Sitenna," he asked me, "were you ever able to attend school?"

"No," I answered. "I was always working."

Dr. Barlow made notes about everything I told him and then asked how he could help me. I asked him to teach me to write.

When I first met Dr. Barlow, he was an elderly man, but he began teaching me to write the Amharic alphabet. He gave me the money I needed to rent a room in Soddo. Daily he made me practice over and over again by copying ten times what he had written in an exercise book. Soon I learned to write my name and other words. I became very close to Dr. Barlow. I even called him my father.

Dr. Barlow gave much thought to what would be the best for me: getting an education or earning money in the marketplace. He decided that I needed schooling. He purchased books so that I could start school. But Dr. Barlow was growing older and weaker.

One day Dr. Barlow's daughter Sharon, her husband Jim, and their son Kevin came to see him. The kind doctor took Jim's and Sharon's hands and asked them to take responsibility for me after he died. Because of his kindness I received money for rent, food, and tuition every month. I also worked for the Mossy Foot Project as the head of the cleaners, and I earned money this way. Jim and Sharon also enrolled me in a private girls' school, which I attended for many years.

Recently I had the joy of being married. Since I considered Sharon a mother to me, I asked her to attend my wedding. Before the ceremony singers and the church congregation came singing and dancing to welcome my groom and me. The pastor preached before the ceremony began, and after we exchanged vows and rings, my husband and I knelt in prayer. I felt so beautiful in my bridal dress—so different from when I used to hide my feet in church.

After the ceremony we enjoyed a happy wedding feast with our friends and neighbors. All the Mossy Foot staff came to celebrate and join in the feast. I was so thankful to God for all His goodness to me that I was even glad to invite the woman who had kicked me out of her house when I became ill with mossy foot disease.

My life was so hard for so many years, but through the kindness of Dr. Kelema and Dr. Barlow and many others, God blessed me in many ways.

God has done such great things in my life that I can never repay Him for His goodness. But I have tried to respond to His kindness toward me by showing kindness to others in need. I raised and educated a poor little girl whose father and mother died. Another little girl lived with me, and I helped her attend school through the fourth grade before her parents took her back.

Yet I could still not pay for all that the Lord has done for me. He has truly seen the need of a small forgotten girl and used the strong and wise to help her.

6

Feleke's Story

suffering for a Purpose

God had a purpose in allowing me to suffer. Out of my experience with mossy foot, God called me to do this work for others.

As the wound-care specialist and healthcare trainer for all sixteen Mossy Foot clinics in Wolaita, Ethiopia, I have the privilege of helping mossy foot patients from all over our region. I love my work, and it is very satisfying for me to help mossy foot sufferers improve. But things weren't always so good for me.

My problem began when I was fifteen years old. Small mossy growths appeared on my feet, and my toes began to swell. My father did not have much money, but he gathered as much as he could and took me to three different hospitals around Arba Minch. I didn't get any relief, however, from the treatments I received.

At that time my feet weren't very bad, but I started to worry when I saw beggars with huge, disfigured feet and oozing ulcers that smelled bad. Would my feet become like theirs someday?

I was eager to go to school, but I was concerned that if my condition worsened, no one would hire me after I finished school, and the expense and time I would spend on an education would be wasted. So I decided not to go to school but to focus my efforts on farming and business instead.

As I became a young man, I wanted to get married. I figured that I'd better hurry and find someone before my feet got worse and no one would marry me. The problem was that many of my neighbors had seen my feet and knew that I had "zoohoenee" disease (mossy foot). How could I get a bride if all the women in my area knew that I had this condition? Because of my dilemma, I moved to an area where no one knew me, and there I kept my feet hidden as best I could.

I was afraid that my feet might become so bad that I couldn't work to support a wife and children, so I decided that I should marry a girl from a rich family. That way if I became incapacitated or died, my family would have someone to take care of them. So I began searching for someone rich to marry.

Before long I found a girl I liked a lot. To make a good impression on her, I bought new shoes, pants, and shirts, and

I groomed myself carefully. I pursued her by buying her gold rings and bracelets. Our courtship was very short: within a month we were married.

It was the custom at that time for a man to feed his new bride very well for two months. I took good care of my wife, and she and I were happy together.

But difficulties were around the corner. I played soccer with some of the local guys, a few of whom were my wife's relatives. As we played one day, they saw my bare feet and realized that something was wrong. Until this point I had concealed my problem at home by waiting until it was dark to take my shoes off. But after this, one day when I wasn't at home, my wife's relatives came by our house and told her about my feet. They tried to persuade her to leave me.

I had discovered that whenever I put my feet up, the swelling lessened, so that night I elevated my feet all night long. The next morning I wore a pair of shorts and sandals in front of my wife so that she would see my legs and feet, now fairly normal in size, and think that they were normal. Since she could see no problem with my feet, she was confused. Why had her relatives wanted her to leave me?

Our first child, a daughter, was born. Soon after that we had a second daughter. My feet were getting bigger and bigger, and they were hurting me very much. After our third child, a son, was born, my condition became even worse.

In desperation I wept and cried out to God, "Please, please help me! I'm afraid my wife will leave me. I don't want to lose my wife and my children." Being frightened and without hope, I decided that my family would be better off without me. If I left them, then my wife's parents, who were well off, could take care of my family. So I went far away to a desert area of Ethiopia.

At this point I considered ending my life. But I was afraid to commit suicide, because I knew that it was a sin. I asked God why He was letting me suffer like this and not answering my prayers.

I didn't know it then, but God was taking care of me. He knew what I was going through and had a plan to help me.

A friend of mine tracked me down and reasoned with me. He told me that my family loved me and missed me very much, and he persuaded me to return to them. When I arrived home, my family was glad to see me.

Soon after I returned to my home, a girl in my neighborhood came to visit me and told me about a doctor in the town of Soddo who was helping people who had the foot condition that I had. This gave me great hope, as I had never heard of someone who could successfully treat this terrible disease. So in the year 2000, I went to find Dr. Barlow to see if he could help me.

Dr. Barlow welcomed me to the clinic and taught me how to care for my feet by applying ointment to them, wrapping them, and elevating them. Within two months I saw a lot of improvement. I was so happy and amazed! By the end of a year of treatment, my feet had returned to good condition.

If I hadn't found treatment when I did, I'm sure that I would be dead today.

Since my feet were now healthy, Dr. Barlow gave me the opportunity to be trained in making shoes. The training lasted two years. When I made shoes, I tried hard to make them as well as I could so that they would be comfortable for the mossy foot patients. I understood the patients' needs and wanted to help them the way I had been helped.

Now the circumstances of my life were completely changed for the better. My feet were in good condition. I had a job making shoes, and I was able to support my family. I was thankful to have a new life and direction for the future.

Six years after I first visited Dr. Barlow and the Mossy Foot Project, as I worked one day, I saw that Lukas, our regular healthcare worker, was sick. I helped out by washing the feet of a patient as he sat outside the clinic. Meskele, the Mossy Foot director, who was working inside, noticed through the window what I was doing and came outside.

"How would you like to change from being a shoemaker to receiving training to be a healthcare worker?" he said to me.

That excited me. "Yes," I told him, "I would like that very much!"

So that is how I came to be trained in Mossy Foot's basic foot treatment. After my initial schooling Robin, an American lady, trained me in lymphatic treatment and wound care. When she returned to Wolaita to do more work with the staff, Robin chose me for further training and taught me to train others.

Today I supervise the healthcare workers at the sixteen Mossy Foot clinics. My work is very rewarding to me. I am content with my salary and with my living conditions. My greatest reward is not in financial gain but in helping other mossy foot patients and seeing them improve. I greatly enjoy helping others get better. I know what the patients are going through, so I can encourage them and give them hope.

I struggled for many years because of my feet, but I know now that God had a purpose in allowing me to get mossy foot disease and to suffer through all the things I went through. He had a plan. I believe that out of my experience with mossy foot, God called me to do this work for others. Now I want to see not just people in the Wolaita region healed from mossy foot disease but also people throughout Ethiopia and in other parts of the world.

God has blessed me and my family in so many ways since I joined the Mossy Foot Project. I am truly grateful.

7

More Changed Lives

Sharon Barlow Daly

His life has turned around—and he hasn't stopped smiling.

Our Toyota Land Cruiser negotiated the steep mountain road, winding back and forth, descending down, down, down to the vast plain of the river valley thousands of feet below. I could see the town in the distance where we had a Mossy Foot clinic. As we pulled into the compound, patients were standing around, awaiting our arrival.

Although Jim and I work from the Unites States, raising funds for the Mossy Foot Project and spreading the news of the ministry, we often travel to Ethiopia to help those serving on the ground and to meet the people who are being helped by the work. How we love carrying on this work that my father started so many years ago!

At each of the sixteen Mossy Foot sites, we are excited to witness firsthand the ongoing expansion of the work. On the opening day of our new clinic in the town of Gale, about five hundred patients came, many of them people who had formerly had to walk several hours to reach one of our other existing clinics. At the Koyo site we observed Matewos, our clinic site director, giving out loans, and then we were invited to go along with Birtukay, who was getting ready to set up her brand-new injera business. We went with her into town, where she bought necessary items, then we went back to her home and enjoyed watching her mix her batter. Since the batter is leavened by wild yeast from the air, we had to come back several days later to see Birtukay bake the injera and sell it at the market.

We have delighted at the joy of little children receiving their first pair of shoes, celebrated with former Mossy Foot patients who are benefiting from vocational training and self-help financial assistance, and been moved to tears at the exuberant rejoicing of widows who have had homes built for them by the joint effort of the Mossy Foot Project and the local church. There is nothing more satisfying—or compelling—for us than to see the light in the faces of people who have gone from being sad and alienated to having purpose and hope.

Tesfaynesh's Story: I Want to Serve Jesus

On the opening day of a new clinic, I met a mother and her precious little girl, Tesfaynesh, about eight or nine years old. Tesfaynesh means "hope." One of this little girl's legs was extremely small, and she had a club foot. The other leg was swollen and had a terrible gaping ulcer. Her mother pleaded with me to get help for her little daughter.

Recently we arranged for Tesfaynesh to go to Soddo Christian Hospital, where she had skin-graft surgery to cover the ulcer.

Tesfaynesh is a bright little girl who wants to go to school when she recovers. She loves Jesus very much and liked going to church when she was able to attend. Sadly, people grew tired of carrying her, so Tesfaynesh now stays home on Sunday. But that doesn't dampen her hope. Despite not being able to attend church, Tesfaynesh sings her favorite songs at home. Tesfaynesh says that she wants to serve Jesus when she is well and can walk again.

Israel's Story: Helped by Kindness

Israel Shiferaw, fourteen years old, was born in the town of Dilla in Sidamo zone. His father joined the military when Israel was very young and never returned, leaving Israel and his mother to manage alone.

Living without his father was difficult for the two of them. They had no other means of economy. As life grew more difficult, Israel's mother married another man and left her son with his grandparents.

Life for Israel grew even harder. His grandparents mistreated him. He was beaten for no reason and given inadequate food. He was forced to work beyond his ability. When Israel could no longer take his grandparents' harshness, he decided to search for another place to stay. But he could find no place to go. As a result, he ended up on the streets.

In order to buy food, Israel carried things for people. At the end of each day he chose the porch of a shop to sleep on.

Sometimes the guards chased him from the porch, and he had to sleep leaning against a wall.

Israel developed mossy foot when he was young. His feet first started to itch, and then they began to swell. Mossy-looking formations developed. Living on the streets made things worse, because Israel was always barefoot. Due to the growing disease, his street friends insulted him. Life for him seemed to grow more and more difficult.

One day, a kind woman from Addis Ababa who walked past Israel noticed him sitting on the street. She felt sad for the young man and wanted to help him. She had been to the town of Soddo for work and had heard about the Mossy Foot Project from a worker there. Paying for Israel's transportation, she brought him to the Mossy Foot clinic in Soddo.

The workers gave Israel a place to stay at the Mossy Foot compound while he was being treated. His feet have greatly improved since he has been to Soddo, giving him the opportunity to hope for a brighter future.

Molise's Story: Giving Back

When Molise was young, her feet started to itch and swell— the first stages of mossy foot disease. Being an attractive young woman with a thriving business—Molise made alcoholic beverages and sold them at the local market—she was able to get married in spite of her progressing disease.

Eventually, however, Molise's feet became so diseased that she was no longer able to walk to the market to conduct her business. But one day she heard good news. A clinic that treated mossy foot disease had opened near the town of Badesa, within walking distance of where she lived. In spite of the condition of her feet, she braved the long walk and trudged to the Mossy Foot clinic. The workers there shared the gospel with Molise, treated her diseased feet, taught her how to care for her feet between clinic visits, and gave her a treatment kit to take home.

Hope rose as Molise faithfully used the kit at home and began noticing improvement in her feet. She returned to the Mossy Foot clinic near Badesa and received a second treatment kit.

But this time upon returning home, her husband was waiting for her. "That smells bad," he cried angrily. With that outcry, Molise's husband grabbed the medicine from her hands, marched outside to the toilet pit, and lobbed it down the deep, dark hole. Molise was devastated. She sobbed and sobbed.

Some time later Mossy Foot opened a new clinic at Kercheche, nearer Molise's house. She went to the Kercheche clinic quietly, without her husband's knowledge. There she got another treatment kit and used it secretly. Without skipping a day of treating her feet, she saw significant improvement.

When Molise's feet were almost well, her husband unexpectedly died.

Molise has a natural talent for business. Now a widow and needing a means of support, she acquired a self-help loan from Mossy Foot and started selling spices and other items at her local outdoor market. From the proceeds of her business, she is raising her children and sending them to school. One of her sons has now graduated and is also working.

Before Molise's husband died, she was not a Christian. Now she has accepted Christ as her Savior and is a church member. She ardently worships the Lord and praises Him for healing her feet and for blessing her business.

This dear lady has chosen to reach out to others. She helps the needy mossy foot patients in her neighborhood through sharing food and clothing with them and encouraging them. She also prays for them and shares the good news of the gospel with them.

Ato Anjulo's Story: Serving God Once Again

Another story we heard as we traveled was that of Ato Anjulo, a pastor who had developed mossy foot disease. As his feet swelled and as large, bumpy growths appeared on his toes, he began to experience discrimination from the church elders. They no longer wanted to eat with Ato Anjulo or wash their feet in the bucket in which he washed his feet. He was insulted and humiliated by his friends and family. People did not want to walk on the road where he walked.

When Ato Anjulo realized that he was being cast out, he came to a decision he had never thought he would make: he decided to stop serving God. Before he developed mossy foot disease, he had been a well-known farmer. But all the time he farmed, he had never worn shoes. None of his family members had had mossy foot disease—but for some reason it started with Ato Anjulo. His feet became so big that they wouldn't fit into the largest shoes sold in town.

For eight long years Ato Anjulo sought treatment from many clinics and doctors. No one was able to help him. When one of his daughters got married, her husband asked her if anyone in her family was a mossy foot patient. Fearing that he would send her away, she told him that no one in her family had mossy foot. After her husband's question, Ato Anjulo's daughter came to her father's home and took him to a new Mossy Foot clinic that had just opened in Bale town.

At the Mossy Foot clinic, Ato Anjulo began to smile. The workers gave him soap, bleach, and Whitfield's ointment. Over the next few months, as he faithfully followed instructions, went regularly to the clinic, and wore shoes, the size of his feet slowly went down. The bad smell and the growths on his feet lessened. Two years after he first visited the Mossy Foot clinic, Ato Anjulo was able to wear normal shoes sold in the market.

Ato Anjulo was highly motivated to start a business but did not have the funds to do so, so he asked a neighbor to loan him the money. The man said that he would loan him the money if he returned fifty birr (about two and a half U.S. dollars) each month for every one hundred birr borrowed.

Ato Anjulo thought he would make enough money to repay him, so he accepted the loan. But the money he made each month was not enough. So the man nagged him and threatened to take him to court or to take his belongings. Because he wasn't able to repay the man, the man took Ato Anjulo's only milk cow, which he had raised as security against hard times.

Hearing that the Mossy Foot Project gave interest-free self-help loans to their patients, Ato Anjulo decided to ask a clinic worker about it. After hearing his story and also his desire to volunteer for Mossy Foot, the project decided to lend him one thousand birr (about fifty U.S. dollars) without interest. The clinic workers asked Ato Anjulo to repay 10 percent of the loan every month.

This loan made it possible for Ato Anjulo to buy food and clothes for himself and his children. Now, in place of the milk cow taken from him, he owns two cows, one of them a milk cow, and many sheep and goats.

People ask Ato Anjulo, "What is the secret of the change in your life?" He tells them that the secret was God and the Mossy Foot Project. His story is exemplified in 2 Corinthians 1:3–4:

> Praise be to the God and Father of our Lord Jesus Christ, the Father of compassion and the God of all comfort, who comforts us in all our troubles, so that we can comfort those in any trouble with the comfort we ourselves receive from God. (NIV)

When he encounters others with mossy foot disease, he takes them to the Mossy Foot clinic. He is a changed man both physically and spiritually. He is once again serving God. His neighbors respect him, and he is back to serving as a pastor at his church.

Indrias's Story: He Hasn't Stopped Smiling

At the Areka clinic Jim and I made the rounds, embracing the precious, forgotten people who have mossy foot disease, bringing them comfort and encouragement. It is our privilege to share the good news of the gospel with them and to tell them of the Great Physician who heals the body and the soul. As we spoke with people, our healthcare worker, Abraham, took me by the hand and led me around a corner to meet Indrias.

Indrias was a teenage boy whose right foot was extremely swollen and disfigured. The swelling extended up the length of his leg into his groin. Indrias also had severe hearing loss.

A few days after we met him at the clinic, we visited Indrias's home in the countryside. We drove for a while, and after the road became impassible, we walked for another hour. Arriving at Indrias's house, my feet were sore from shoes that weren't made for hiking. The walk back made me think of the dedication Indrias, and many like him, have in order to walk long distances to a clinic so that they can get better.

We brought this young man to our Mossy Foot headquarters in Soddo town so that he could receive daily treatment. There he was fitted with hearing aids by Bill Austin, founder and owner of Starkey Hearing Foundation, who was visiting the Mossy Foot ministry. At our headquarters Indrias also received daily treatments from Feleke, our wound-care and lymphatic specialist. For several months he stayed at our headquarters in Soddo, receiving daily treatments for his foot and leg. His foot improved dramatically, but the swelling in his groin did not respond to the treatment and required care beyond what we could provide.

A generous donor offered to pay for Indrias's medical treatment at a hospital in Tel Aviv, Israel. Since Indrias came straight from the countryside and spoke no English, Pastor Zewdie accompanied him to Israel. Following a successful surgery, Indrias and Pastor Zewdie returned to Ethiopia. Indrias is currently living at the Mossy Foot headquarters in Soddo so that Feleke can give him follow-up treatments. Indrias can now attend school for the first time in his life.

Indrias's life has turned around—and he hasn't stopped smiling.

Epilogue

Take a moment and picture your son or your daughter or your friend's child sloughing through a muddy field after a heavy rain. They trudge over rocks and thorns, their feet cozily protected by thick-soled galoshes or well-padded running shoes.

Now imagine the same child on a five-mile walk, over the same ground—barefoot.

Unthinkable?

Unfortunately, for thousands of children, men, and women who farm in the miry red volcanic clay soil of Ethiopia's highlands, this is not imagination. This is their everyday reality.

Many of our patients cope with severe physical discomfort, but the stigma and rejection that come with disfigured feet frequently are even more painful. In Ethiopia, to live with mossy foot is to be an outcast from society—to be treated as a leper. Many patients have been abandoned by family members.

The problem is that many people in Ethiopia, particularly those in rural areas, are too poor to afford shoes, which would prevent them from getting mossy foot disease.

However, *there is good news!*

Today the Mossy Foot Project operates sixteen clinics in various sites throughout Wolaita zone, Ethiopia. We treat as many as three thousand patients in a month at these sixteen sites. Our healthcare and social/gospel agents are former patients who have been successfully treated. Because of their personal understanding of mossy foot disease, these men and women bring comfort to the people they serve, working tirelessly at the clinics and making home visits to those who are unable to walk to the clinic.

At each of our sites, we offer our patients holistic care. We give each patient the opportunity to be encouraged and inspired with hope for healing and life transformation. We treat each one for mossy foot disease, and we educate people as to the cause of the disease and the proper care of their feet. We give patients treatment kits to use at home and a pair of oversized custom leather shoes, which are manufactured by former patients. Our clients are expected to pay 10 percent of the cost of treatment if they can afford to do so.

Now that we are seeing such tremendous improvement in our patients' feet, we are able to focus on their economic recovery as well. Helping people to become financially independent will enable them to buy shoes for themselves and their children in the future. Consequently, we have begun granting small loans to eligible patients. In order to quality for this self-help assistance, the individual needs letters of recommendation and must pass a foot inspection by Feleke, our wound-care and lymphatic specialist, to ensure that he or she is well enough to successfully conduct a business. The average loan is between eighty-five and one hundred dollars. We have a very good record of the loans being repaid in the first year. As of summer 2012 we had given out over nine hundred self-help assistance loans to patients whose feet had been successfully treated.

Vocational training for young men and women is another way we assist our patients in becoming financially self-sufficient. Mossy Foot offers training in shoemaking, carpentry, bike repair, radio repair, hairdressing, and barber work. Participants in this program live at our headquarters in Soddo for a month, where they receive training. Upon graduation they are issued a tool kit, and they return to their villages and set up their own businesses, most of which have been quite successful! So far approximately two hundred people have received vocational training.

In 2010 the Mossy Foot Project began building homes for widows and abandoned women who are patients at the clinics. Due to lack of education about mossy foot disease, the family members of affected individuals often believe that they are contagious and no longer valuable to society. Women are especially vulnerable and are often abandoned by their husbands. These women are left with no shelter, no food, and no care. Many times they have children to support as well. The homes built for these patients are modest, but they provide a suitable shelter to protect these women and children from the rainy weather and the hyenas that are prevalent in Ethiopia. Often Mossy Foot Project partners with the local church and other community groups in the construction. We provide the metal roofing and nails, and the church provides the framework and labor. The joy released when the community comes together to help a destitute widow with a new home is palpable.

With so many of our patients' feet now being in quite good condition, we are ready to expand again to outlying regions where others suffering from mossy foot disease have not yet had the opportunity to be treated. Our goal is to expand the number of Mossy Foot Project clinics to a total of thirty. We desire to grow our prevention program and increase the distribution of shoes and socks to our patients, and we want to provide literacy education for children and young adults impacted by mossy foot disease. Please pray for the Mossy Foot ministry as we continue to reach out to those who are in need.

"Jesus went through all the towns and villages, teaching in their synagogues, proclaiming the good news of the kingdom and healing every disease and sickness" (Matt. 9:35, NIV).

More About the Mossy Foot Project
Frequently Asked Questions

Why Ethiopia?

Ethiopia is one of the African countries most heavily affected by mossy foot disease. An estimated 1 million Ethiopians, mostly subsistence farmers, are infected. In 2005 the disease was estimated to cost Wolaita zone (an area of 1.5 million people) 16 million dollars per year. In areas with irritant soil and subsistence farming, up to 5 percent of the population may be affected, making mossy foot even more common than HIV in these areas.

The Mossy Foot Project is headquartered in the city of Soddo, home to eighty-six thousand people, within Wolaita zone. It is a five-hour drive south from the capital city of Addis Ababa. All sixteen Mossy Foot clinics are in Wolaita zone. The need for treatment of mossy foot disease beyond Soddo, however, is great.

- Ethiopia has a population of 94 million people; 44 percent of these are children under the age of fifteen.

- There is one doctor for every forty thousand people.

- On the United Nations Human Development index, Ethiopia ranks in the bottom fifteen of the poorest countries in the world.

- Less than 40 percent of the adult population can read and write.

- 85 percent of workers are involved in agriculture.

- These factors contribute to the high incidence of mossy foot and the great need for education and medical care.

What exactly does Mossy Foot do?

The Mossy Foot Project is a faith-based Christian organization that works to raise the level of awareness about mossy foot disease in the Western world and works toward the prevention, treatment, and eradication of the disease among those who are at risk in Ethiopia.

We provide medical treatment, education, vocational training, and social counseling to individuals and their families who are afflicted with mossy foot disease.

Mossy Foot Project takes a holistic approach to addressing this disease by providing care for the whole person. Along with offering physical care and education to reduce symptoms, we also provide vocational training to assist families in establishing a means for their livelihood, and we offer recovering patients self-help financial assistance so that they can start businesses to support themselves. In addition, the love and encouragement extended to our patients brings transforming power to their lives.

How is the Mossy Foot Project structured?

The Mossy Foot Project has been registered as a 501(c)3 non-profit organization in the United States since 2006 and a chartered NGO (non-governmental organization) in Ethiopia since 2000. In Ethiopia, the organization operates under the name Mossy Foot International.

Our U.S. office is located in Ventura, California, and is headed by Sharon Daly (president) and Jim Daly (vice president), the daughter and son-in-law of Dr. Nathan Barlow, founder of the Mossy Foot Project. Renee Hrabak also works in the Ventura office as the project treasurer.

In Ethiopia key positions are held by Yoseph Menna, national representative and executive director, Mebrat Borku, social work coordinator, Feleke Kolcha, wound-care and lymphatic specialist, and Matewos Hilo, clinic site director.

The Mossy Foot Project also has a wonderful board of directors that offers diverse skills and backgrounds and provides oversight and input for the direction of the organization.

How do Mossy Foot clinics function?

The Mossy Foot Project has sixteen clinics in the Wolaita zone of Ethiopia, each one staffed by two indigenous workers—former mossy foot patients—who treat mossy foot disease as well as do social work. Each clinic treats over two hundred patients every month. Patients who seek help from the Mossy Foot clinics are offered help in a variety of ways:

- Treatment, which includes soaking, applying ointment, and bandaging, and education so that patients can care for their feet at home

- Referral to hospital for surgery in cases beyond our ability to help

- Distribution of socks and shoes, and education as to the benefits of wearing them

- Vocational training, including the making of large shoes to fit mossy foot patients, hairdressing, bicycle maintenance, masonry, carpentry, poultry farming, and healthcare

- Self-help financial assistance to provide former patients with the means to become financially self-sufficient

- Emotional and social support through the clinic workers and volunteers who were former patients

- Building of homes for widows and abandoned women who have become outcasts due to mossy foot disease

What are your plans for the future?

We have a number of plans for the future of the Mossy Foot Project:

- Move into new areas of Wolaita as well as expand into other regions throughout Ethiopia where mossy foot sufferers have not yet received help

- Expand the shoemaking program and the distribution of shoes and socks to mossy foot patients

- Expand our children's shoe distribution program for children of families that have been affected by mossy foot disease (preventive training and care)

- Continue to graduate patients whose feet are in good condition and who can now take care of themselves so that we can extend our care to those who have not yet received help

- Provide literacy education for children and young adults who have been impacted by mossy foot disease

- Expand our vocational training program

- Continue our self-help assistance program

Another exciting development is our building project. Several years back the Ethiopian government designated a parcel of land for use by the Mossy Foot Project to develop a campus for administration, treatment, training, and research. It is located in the north section of Soddo, Ethiopia, along a main road.

This will increase our capacity to serve those in need and enable us to expand vocational training for our healed and healing mossy foot patients so that they can increase their standard of living.

The initial work of building a surrounding wall and gate, a pit latrine, and a guard house is now complete. Further development of the property will include multiple phases:

- Phase I: move the Mossy Foot headquarters onto the property. The headquarters will include a greeting area, offices, clinic, storage area, large multi-purpose room (for meetings and training), shoe-making room, bathrooms, two guest rooms, and a small kitchen.

- Phase II: expand services provided in the area of shoemaking and vocational training and provide support for these activities through a dormitory, wash room, kitchen facilities, etc.

- Phase III: add two housing units for visiting expatriate workers.

We praise God for supplying funds for phase I of our training center and headquarters. Our big need now is for more monthly partners so that we can expand the clinic outreach and treatment. Our project architect has developed an attractive and flexible design, and we are ready to build as funds become available.

How can I get involved?

First and foremost, you can pray. As E. M. Bounds said, "Prayer breaks all bars, dissolves all chains, opens all prisons, and widens all straits by which God's saints have been held."

- Pray for the people of Ethiopia and the ability of the Mossy Foot Project to help meet all their needs.

- Pray for people's increasing awareness of the work of Mossy Foot so that more will volunteer and give.

- Pray for God's provision of resources so that we can continue building our permanent headquarters in Soddo, Ethiopia.

- Pray for wisdom for our board of directors and officers so that they will guide the work along a fruitful path.

- Pray for trustworthy and compassionate workers to lead the activity and to care for the patients in Ethiopia.

- Pray that our patients will experience the transformational love and care that will forever change their lives.

You can donate. Ninety-nine percent of Mossy Foot Project costs are met by donations from partner churches and individuals. Without our partners it would not be possible to keep this vital project operating.

You can like us on Facebook.

You can download the Mossy Foot brochure at www.mossyfoot.com/wp-content/uploads/2013/10/Mossy-Foot-Brochure.pdf and share it with others.

You can read and subscribe to the Mossy Foot newsletter at http://mossyfoot.com/our-stories/newsletter-archive.

You can educate yourself about mossy foot disease and the Mossy Foot Project by reading our website and blog at www.mossyfoot.com. In addition to gaining information, you can find many more stories like the ones you have read in this book, and you can also view photos of Zelalem, Megiso, Sitenna, and others.

You can host an event to spread the news about the Mossy Foot Project.

You can hold a fundraiser for the Mossy Foot Project.

If you, your church small group, your church, or other group are interested in obtaining more information on how to get involved with the Mossy Foot Project, please get in touch with us (contact information is listed at the end of this section).

OUR VISION, MISSION, AND PURPOSE

Vision
A world free of mossy foot disease

Mission
Providing mossy foot patients with life-changing resources
through medical treatment, prevention, education, vocational
training, and a message of eternal hope

Purpose
To eliminate mossy foot disease while sharing God's love

GET IN TOUCH WITH US

E-mail: info@mossyfoot.com
Website: www.mossyfoot.com
Write: P.O. Box 5311 Ventura, CA 93005
Call: 855-996-6779